The Ar

MW00929742

How to Make Better Choices in Love, Life, and Work

By Madison Taylor

Copyright 2016 by Madison Taylor

Published by Make Profits Easy LLC

Profitsdaily123@aol.com

facebook.com/MakeProfitsEasy

Table of Contents

Chapter 1: Introduction

Have you ever grappled with a decision? The answer is almost certainly yes. Everyone has dealt with a tough decision during at least one point in life. Some decisions are hard to make because both options seem equal. Other decisions are difficult because you must choose a lesser evil. And yet others are hard because you simply do not want to make them.

You may find that the process of reaching decisions makes you ache with anxiety. It may seem impossible for you to decide on things, even simple things, like what to eat for dinner. You may be the type who spends twenty minutes staring at the menu at a restaurant, terrified that if you choose the wrong dish you will suffer tremendously throughout the entire meal. Decisions are not easy for you; in fact, they cause you a great deal of misery. If you are this type of person who struggles with indecision, then this book is for you. You can learn the fine art of making decisions without all the anxiety and heartache.

Decisions are so important. Every day you must decide between two or more options. Sometimes the decisions you face are dire, and other times they are not so significant. Nevertheless, you must make the right decision to avoid all the consequences of making the wrong one. This can boil down to life or death in some situations. In others, it is really not so dire, but you might feel like it is.

Fear of making the wrong decision can paralyze you and put you in a frantic state of anxiety that does not benefit anyone. You feel stuck and you wonder if you are about to end your life or someone else's. You waver like a leaf about to fall off of a tree in autumn, too scared to take the plunge but unable to hang on anymore either. Sadly, sometimes in life, snap decisions are necessary. Dire situations and certain jobs require you to have confidence in deciding things expediently. Sitting around paralyzed in fear and uncertainty really does you no good.

Learning how to make wise decisions helps you govern your life better. You can pick the directions you need to go without making mistakes. You can practice discernment and prevent unwise choices. You can even start making snap decisions in emergencies or in your career. Above all, your confidence and wisdom will make you stand out and grant you more power over others.

Decision making is an art. Just as practice makes your drawing better or your free throws more precise, practice can greatly improve your ability to make wise decisions. Learning to use wisdom and finesse in making a decision or judgment call is something that you must learn. When you know how to make wise decisions, your anxiety lessens. The time it takes you to make a decision also lessens. Life becomes better as you are able to navigate it more wisely and choose the proper courses of action.

In the following chapters, you will learn the skills necessary for wise decision making.

You will be handed all the tools needed to perform this art. But this book is not your only guide. You must apply these concepts and practice them to get better at decision making. This book is a wonderful start, but improvement in your decision making abilities is up to you entirely.

It is only through your own efforts that you can become a master of decision making. You need to implement these tips to enjoy success in decision making. Then, you need to practice avidly. The work will pay off because you will no longer feel agony when faced with an important decision. You will have the faculties to make appropriate decisions without serious unpleasant repercussions. Your life will greatly benefit overall.

Chapter 2: How to Make Good Decisions

To make a good decision, you need to change your thinking a little bit. Right now, you probably suffer from negative thinking patterns that render you indecisive. Your thought habits restrict you from taking the proper attitude toward healthy, wise decision making. There can be a few major causes of your indecisiveness, which you can easily correct just by adjusting your mental state a little bit.

Define a Good Decision

What is a good decision? A good decision is ideally the choice that offers you the most benefits with the least associated risks. A good decision does not hurt you or others. Ultimately, it will solve the issues that you are trying to overcome.

There is a difference between a good decision and the best decision. A good decision is satisfactory and adequate. The best decision is just that, the best option available. You want to strive for the best decision possible. But sometimes a good decision is enough. Do not put too much pressure on yourself to reach the perfect decision when a good decision is adequate.

When you understand what a good decision is, you are better able to make one. Set clear criteria for what you want. Then make sure that your decision meets your criteria as much as possible. You should compare every option you have to your list of criteria so that you can find which one serves you the best in the end.

Leave it to Chance

The first reason that you are indecisive is that you may feel overly controlling of your life. Many people think they need to control every aspect of life. But this is simply not true. Many things do not even require for you to make a decision. Sometimes you need to relinquish control. Ask yourself, does something really need you to get involved? Do you really need to make a decision?

Sometimes it far easier to leave things to chance. Life will often make decisions for you if you just relax and let things work out the way that they are meant to. Not taking action is sometimes the best action. When you do not take action, people and things that are not meant for you will move on. You will miss the opportunity because of your inaction, but this is a good thing. The things and people that stick around are often the ones that you should choose. They are meant to be.

Certainly you do not want to use inaction all of the time. Sometimes things really do call for a decision on your part. If you really want something or if a decision is life or death, you need to act.

Remove the Fear

You may also be indecisive because you put too much importance on a decision. The decision equals life or death to you. You are terrified of making the wrong choice and ruining everything. This form of thinking is known as catastrophizing. If you are filled with anxiety whenever you make a decision, you may just suffer from catastrophizing. Ask yourself when you are trying to make a decision, what is the worst that could happen if you make the wrong choice? Will it really ruin your life?

Sometimes, a bad decision can be totally devastating. But in many cases, the repercussions of the wrong choice are easily solvable. It is quite possible to recover from the fallout of a wrong decision. So when you are faced with a decision, consider how bad the repercussions could possibly be. Asking yourself this can help you realize that some decisions are not worth agonizing over. Then, you will feel more comfortable making a choice without the paralysis of fear. You will feel confident that you can survive the repercussions either way, and you do not hesitate anymore.

You should remove the fear out of all decisions that you make. Even life or death decisions, which can certainly be scary, should be turned into logical equations in your mind. That makes dire decisions so much easier to make. Adding fear to the decision making process usually just makes the decision absolutely paralyzing.

Take Your Time

Some decisions call for snappy decision making. I will cover how to make quick decisions later. However, a majority of decisions do not require for a rapid judgment call. You can remove the panic from making a decision by giving yourself some time. Breathe and turn your brain off for a second, rather than frantically dashing around trying to decide something quickly.

Look at a decision. Does it really need to be made right now? Can you safely sleep on it? If so, then by all means take your time. Taking your time lets you make a more informed decision. Do not spend this time avoiding thinking about your decision, however. Definitely be proactive and perform research to help you reach the decision you need to make.

Follow Your Heart

This is the oldest advice in the book. When you learn to listen to your heart, you will find that it makes the best decisions for you. Your heart is aware of what makes you happy. When you listen to it, it will guide you to the decision that you really wanted to make. If you are indecisive, one cause may be that you ignore your heart.

The clutter in your brain can make it almost impossible to hear what your heart is saying to you. Therefore, it can be helpful to employ certain tricks. For instance, try flipping a coin. If you are not happy with the results, then you just heard your heart. Go with the decision that you secretly wanted the coin to direct you to.

Remove the Permanence

You can take the fear out of many decisions by removing the permanence from them. While some decisions are very final, most are not. It is often possible to change your mind about something if you realize that you made the wrong decision.

If you make a decision, try to stick with it. You never know how something will work out in the end if you do not give it time. When you become antsy about a decision, try to remind yourself why you made it in the first place. This can help you stick to it.

However, if you are totally sure that something was a mistake, then it is better to act quickly. The minute you make a decision and you sense that it is not working out, take action to run damage control. Make it known to others that you are not happy with your choice. Do what you need to do to implement changes immediately. The sooner you act, the less likely you are to get buried over your head and totally stuck in a decision.

A common example of this is returning a purchase. Do not wait. Make the return immediately before it expires or you accidentally damage the merchandise. If you hire someone that you regret, you should quickly terminate the contract and hire someone better.

Sometimes, it may take a while to be able to change your decision. If you decide poorly on a college choice, you can always switch, but you may have to wait until enrollment reopens at a different college. If you choose the wrong job, you may have to stick it out for a while until you find something better. Waiting can make the bad decision seem fatal, but really it is not. Usually, life is long enough that a few bad decisions do not mean you never have a chance to right them. Even if you have to wait a while, you will have learned a valuable lesson and you still have the opportunity to change your mind.

If you cannot change your mind for whatever reason, make the best of the bad consequences. They may provide a valuable learning experience.

Once you make a decision, you will have to live with the consequences. But keep in mind that in many cases, you can change the consequences if you do not like them. It is always possible to make another decision or to change your mind later on.

Understand You are not Exempt from Failure

No one is ever exempt from failure. Even the best decision can yield poor results. While this idea may strike you with fear, you should not let it. Instead, use this idea to understand that the decision you make now may not matter so much in the long run. You may face failure or bad results no matter what decision you make. Do not put all of your faith in one decision and do not think that all of your life rides on making the right or wrong decision right now. Focus more on fixing mistakes once they happen, rather than preventing them right off the bat by making the perfect decision.

Of course, you do not want to recklessly make bad decisions, thinking that you can just clean up your messes later. This is not at all what I mean. What I mean is, do not put too much pressure on yourself to make the perfect decision right this instant. You should try to make the best decision possible, but do not worry incessantly that you will mess your whole life up if you accidentally make the wrong decision. You may have to deal with undesirable consequences from either decision that you make, so relax a little bit.

Have a Fallback

You can lessen the severity of a bad decision by always creating a good fallback option. Your fallback is another option or course of action that you can take should your original option not work out to your satisfaction. Fallback options keep you safe and they make you feel safe, as well.

For instance, when you apply to jobs or colleges, apply to your first choices. Without a doubt, you want to try for what you want the most. But also apply to lesser jobs or schools just in case you don't get into your primary choice.

A fallback option can really save you. But more than anything, appreciate the security it gives you. That security can give you the confidence you need to go after your dreams without fear because you know that no matter what, you will come out OK.

Weigh Pros and Cons

Weighing pros and cons can make a decision more logical. Instead of just blindly trying to make a decision, you can calmly sit down with a pen and paper and create a list of the pros and cons. Find out all the good things and bad things. Jot them down in two separate columns for both choices. If the cons outnumber the pros for a certain choice, then clearly that choice is not worthy and you should go with the other option.

You can also rate pros and cons, since some will have greater importance than others. Rate the least important pros and cons as one, and increase the importance numerically. When you have completed your list, add up the pros in one column and the cons in another for all of your choices. The choice with the highest numerical value of pros is the choice you should go with.

Map out Decisions on Paper

It is a great idea to create a decision tree. A decision tree is a rather complex graph but it can make decision making simpler. For each decision, you can draw branches that show predictable outcomes and the pros and cons. From this tree, you can draw conclusions about which decision offers the best possible outcomes and the most pros. The tree is very helpful because it lets you view the decision objectively. But it is also helpful because it enables you to come up with new points as you go along. You will notice and think of things that never occurred to you in the confusion of your own brain.

Force field analysis is another way to map out a decision. You analyze the forces that work for and against each proposed change. You can analyze what will go into implementing a decision.

Map out each decision you grapple with in these different ways to remove yourself from the decision and think about it with more clarity. A decision will seem less threatening and overwhelming when it is laid out on paper. You will be able to approach it more objectively. You can also see its different outcomes, pros and cons, and forces with more clarity, which can make the decision making process much easier.

Do your Research

Do your research so that you can feel confident about all of your decisions. You can learn the real pros and cons that will enable you to make an educated decision. Make sure to gather research from all the most unbiased sources and look well into both the good and the bad.

This can be especially helpful when you are making a decision about something such as what school to go to, what job to accept, or what area or city to move to. You will be able to find a wealth of information about all of your options online and from people who have already attended, worked at, or lived in your difference choices. Do not be afraid to approach people and ask for their input. Visit online discussion boards.

You should also perform this research on products, vehicles, and other purchases. Never just rely on advertising because companies will only show their best assets and hide their worst flaws in ads. You can find a wealth of product reviews, safety ratings, and other information online.

When hiring people or choosing a company to do business with, look at such sites as Angie's List and Ripoff Report. Do your research very carefully about the people and companies that you are interested in.

You can benefit a great deal from doing research. Once you have some sound knowledge under your belt, you can feel more secure about making a decision. Often the information you dig up will make a decision for you.

Reframe Decisions into Positives

Reframing the way you think about the decisions that you make is important. Changing the way you think about your choices makes it easier to stop viewing them as terrible or dire undertakings. Add positivity to decisions.

Don't think "I hate both choices" but instead "I love this about this choice" and base a decision off of what you love. Look at the good in each choice and determine which one offers you more benefits in the end, rather than which one will hurt you the most.

Focusing on the good rather than the bad can make decisions seem better and easier to make. You are no longer basing your choice off of fear, which can be restricting and anxiety-provoking, but instead base them off of love and benefit. You will feel better about the outcomes, too, and you will look forward to reaping the rewards of your excellent decision.

Don't Problem Solve

Every decision does not need to be made to solve problems. Stop thinking about how to best solve a problem. Focus only on the decision at hand. This lessens the severity that you assign the decision, which makes the decision making process easier.

This may seem counterintuitive. Often, you are trying to make a decision to solve a problem. However, it is best to just not think about the problem you are trying to solve. You are already aware of the problem at hand and the decisions that can offer you helpful solutions. So there is no need to keep dwelling on the problem.

Instead think only of the benefits and risks of the decisions that you are now faced with.

Be Independent

Your decisions are your own to make. Do not let other people influence your decision. The opinions and advice of other people will only confuse you and make it harder for you to listen to your own heart and reason. In addition, if you make the opposite decision of what someone advised, that person may become annoyed or even upset with you for not following his advice.

Tune out Mental Chatter

Sometimes, while making a decision, it can seem like a million voices rise up in your head. They distract you and confuse you. It is impossible to make a decision with so much chatter going on in your head. Turning off these thoughts is essential to being able to calmly approach decision making.

When these thoughts start, switch them off by focusing instead on something else. Try a mindfulness meditation where you focus on just the rhythm of your breathing in and out to quiet your mind. You can also try yoga nidra or progressive muscle relaxation. Both train you to focus on tensing and relaxing certain muscles throughout your body so that your thoughts turn away from distraction and instead become focused on your physical state. Do whatever it takes to remove the excessive thinking from a decision.

Be a Satisficer

What is that word, satisficer? It is a term supported by Barry Schwartz in *The Paradox of Choice*. Schwartz found that there are two groups of decision makers. Satisficers set criteria, and once that criteria is met, they are content. They like to make adequate decisions. Maximizers will not stop looking for the optimal option, even once they have found something satisfactory. They want to keep searching for a better choice. Satisficers are generally happier and enjoy more ease making decisions, Schwartz found.

As a result of these findings, Schwartz surmises that satisficers are generally better off. You should be content with the adequate decision. Obsessively performing research to maximize the benefits of your decision can drive you crazy and cost you your happiness. It can also turn decision making into a stressful ordeal.

Think of Gain, Not Loss

In a study, people were exposed to stressors, such as making a speech or plunging their hands into ice water. Then, they were asked to make decisions while their brains were still under the influence of stress hormones from these activities. Through this study, a great deal was discovered about reaching decisions. Interestingly, one of the main findings was that when people are faced with some sort of gain, they act more conservatively in their decisions. Meanwhile, when faced with loss, people make riskier decisions. This is probably because people feel more reckless and panicked when they are about to lose something versus when they are about to gain something.

To ensure that you make wiser decisions, being conservative can be helpful. Therefore, try your best to frame your decision in terms of gain rather than loss. Don't worry about what you are going to lose if you make one decision or another. Instead, consider what you will gain. Will you gain more money? Better opportunities? Better health?

Weighing the Risks

It is nice and even helpful to focus on the good rather than the bad when making a decision. But some decisions call for you to find the lesser or more mitigable risk, rather than the greater benefit.

Say you have a serious health complication and you are trying to choose between two different procedures that both have high rates of success. You are likely to get well if you choose either procedure, which means that the benefit is exactly the same. But one procedure carries the high risk of kidney failure and you may have to be on dialysis for the rest of your life. The other procedure carries the risk of a stroke that could kill you. Now you must choose which risk you would prefer to deal with. Some people may prefer dying over being on dialysis, while others might prefer surviving and dealing with dialysis. Everyone is different.

When a decision poses the same benefit but different risks, you must think about the long-term. Which risk can you actually see yourself accepting? Which risk will bring you the least pain in the long run? Weigh the risks in situations where you must choose the lesser of two evils.

Chapter 3: Making Decisions under Pressure

While the tips in the previous chapter are great for daily decision making, they often require you to take some time. What do you do if you have no time? What if you are under intense pressure to make a decision quickly? What if this is a stressful life-or-death situation?

Some of the hardest decisions we have to make under pressure have to do with our futures. Our health, our finances, our families, and other things that are deeply important to us call for our decision making. But these decisions create a massive amount of pressure because they are so dire to our survival and our future happiness.

Pressure can make decision making so much harder. But unfortunately, there will be times when you must make decisions under pressure. Life has an overwhelmingly high number of circumstances where decisions must be made quickly, with little time for deliberation and debate. You must learn how to not let pressure get to you and make you indecisive. How is this possible?

Making decisions under pressure calls for you to ignore the pressure. Let your mind stay strong, and don't melt or break under the intense pressure of time and urgency. Read on for tips on how to clear your mind and make a wise decision without the luxury of time.

How to Trust Your Gut

The most obvious answer is to trust your gut. But trusting your gut is not as simple as it sounds. If you are indecisive by Nature, then you obviously have issues just listening to your gut. You would not be reading this book if gut decisions were a skill that you can simply access whenever you need it.

Trusting your gut basically means listening to your own intuition. Everyone is inherently intuitive. But many people do not understand that there are three different types of intuition. Accessing your intuition may become easier if you learn which intuition to draw from. Also, keep in mind that pressure can make your mind work faster. Your intuition is a result of your mind performing at its peak, so your intuition is usually right.

Ordinary intuition is your basic gut instinct. It is your natural first choice. It is the voice in your head that says, "Do this, not that." There is usually no reasoning or thought behind this intuition. It simply seems to appear out of nowhere. In actuality, it does not appear from nowhere, but rather it emerges from complex thought processes and understanding that goes on in the deep subconscious of your mind. This is why your intuition is typically right.

If you ever hear this little voice speak up, it is wise to listen. Your mind might flood with doubt. "Is this really the right option? What about...?" you may ask yourself. But do not question your gut instinct. Always listen to it.

Strategic intuition is a little slower. It is just like ordinary intuition in that it will come to you out of nowhere, like a clear lightning flash, or a light bulb going off. But usually this intuition takes a while to occur. It is because the decision making is going on in the back of your mind, without your conscious involvement. You should also always follow what these flashes of insight tell you to do. This intuition is certainly enlightening, but it is not always useful when you are under the pressure of time.

Expert intuition arises when you are familiar with someone. This is the kind of intuition that might guide you in your career. You are trained and experienced in situations relating to your career, to the point where you are literally an expert. When a decision-making situation arises, you are prepared. You know exactly what decision to make based on your accumulated expertise. When you are experienced in something, listen to your expert intuition. You know more than you give yourself credit for. If your mind immediately retrieves a decision, go with that decision. Your subconscious has the appropriate knowledge to make the decision based on your experience and knowledge, without you having to spend time thinking.

Sometimes, you do not have a clear intuitive voice speak to you right away. When this happens, you should rely on either strategic intuition or expert intuition. But what happens if you don't have any expert intuition either, and you do not have time for strategic intuition to take place in the back of your mind? Then you do have to commit a little bit of conscious effort to the decision making process.

Commit to the Decision

Once you have realize that you have no idea what decision to make, you need to soundly and firmly commit to the process of making a decision within a certain period of time. This commitment helps anchor you to the decision making process so that you actually dedicate time and effort to the decision. You are not going to leave the decision up to fate or up to other people. You are the one who is going to make it.

Now you need to take some steps to make the best decision possible.

Know the Situation

Even when you are under pressure, it is a good idea to ask for a little time to get all the facts straight. You want to know the situation inside and out. You want all of the details. You do not need hours to gather all of the details, but at least take a few minutes to get to know the situation really well.

It is a good idea to ask questions that are designed to cull as much information as possible in a short period of time. Do not ask meandering questions. Rather, ask direct ones about the details that you know you need to make an informed decision.

Employ research if you must. What option is the best? You do not want to make the wrong decision, so you should not let pressure make you neglect to check your facts. However, remember to be a satisficer, not a maximizer. There is no point doing so much research that you confuse yourself. Find out what you need to know to make an informed choice and cut the research off there. Do not go overboard.

With all of the details in place, you are better able to make an informed and educated decision. Knowledge is power when it comes to decision making. Have all the knowledge you can gather to make a proper decision.

Prediction

You cannot predict the future, people say, and they are somewhat right. But with life experience comes a certain ability to recognize patterns and learn from the past. You are better able to predict the outcomes of your decisions than people give you credit for. You can usually have a reasonable prediction about what your different outcomes will be. Use your ability to predict outcomes to determine which decision will have the best results.

It is a good idea to not focus on the negative when predicting outcomes. You can bring a sense of doom into the decision-making process if you focus on which outcome will be worse. Instead, think of which outcome is better. Focus on the benefits and the pros rather than the harms and the cons.

Also, focus on the long-term. Some short-term strife may be better if it avoids long-term problems. Do not make a decision based solely on the short-term benefits that you can see. Use your knowledge of the decision to try to forecast far into the future. It is not always possible to understand the far-reaching implications of your decisions, so sometimes the short-term is all you have to work with. But at least try to keep your scope as long-term as possible.

Good leaders make decisions based on the far future. They understand that a decision that benefits only the short-term will create more problems to fix later on. It is far easier to prevent those problems by focusing on the long-term. Leaders employ strategic decision-making, where their decisions are designed to solve as many problems as possible. They see more than what is before them right now. Many people focus only on the short-term and instant gratification, and they despise good leaders for decisions that do not seem to be wise at first.

Many people fail to realize that the short-term is not as important and that a larger strategy is in the works.

Keep this strategy in mind. Focus on the long-term over the short-term always. Do not worry about what other people see; if a decision creates short-term problems but benefits everyone more in the long-term, then make that decision, and deal with the consequences now rather than later. People may judge you and call you foolish, but they simply do not understand the greater good that you are concerning yourself with. There is wisdom to your decision that others cannot be expected to understand immediately.

Get Advice

Usually, it is advisable to make decisions on your own. Other opinions can only distract you and confuse you. However, at certain times, expert opinions and objective outside perspectives can be crucial. You sometimes need a second pair of eyes to help you see a situation in the proper perspective. This is why businesses often rely on outside consultants for advice on how to approach certain business and financial situations and dilemmas.

Ask people who are not biased by personal involvement in your decision. Ask experts, or objective friends. Really listen to and derive value from their input.

However, the opinion of an objective source is not always right. It can be helpful to ask people for input. But sometimes the reason that this is helpful is because it helps you see how right your own intuition is. If someone suggests a decision that does not jive well with your heart, then by all means, do not take the advice. You are not obligated to make a choice based on someone's input. The decision is still yours to make. Go with the choice that feels best to you. Be sure to always thank other parties for their help, however. You do not want anyone to feel unappreciated if you go against their advice, or they may not want to help you again in the future.

Run Risk Analysis

Do a very quick risk analysis in your head. Jot your thoughts down on a piece of paper if that helps. What are the biggest risks to each decision? Which risk can you live with? Think about this carefully, but a decision will probably become clear to you very quickly. There are some risks that you just cannot deal with. Then there are others that you can. You will know once you conduct a risk analysis.

Risk analysis does not have to take a long time. You can conduct one mentally very quickly and easily. Focus on only one decision at a time to prevent confusion. Writing it down really can make it easier to organize your thoughts, too, and to keep from forgetting key points that you come up with.

When thinking of risks, it helps to rate them. What is the likelihood of the risk? There is risk in everything. A comet might strike the earth and we will die in the subsequent apocalypse; there is always that risk lingering, I suppose. But what is the likelihood of that risk occurring and affecting your life? Not very high, probably. Some risks you think of are not at all likely to occur, while others are almost guaranteed. Rating the likelihood of risks helps you evaluate their level of impact and relevance.

Communicate

Communicate your thought process with the people who also involved in the decision. Good communication helps people understand where you are coming from and why you reached the decision that you did. It helps people prepare for the potential fallout from your decision. You will have a team of people ready to help you deal with the consequences of either decision that you make.

It is especially helpful to rely on your spouse or your family as your support team when it comes to major, stressful decisions. People make the mistake of thinking, "I don't want to worry my husband/wife about this. He/she has enough on his/her plate." But your spouse or family may wind up with even more on their plates if you do not communicate. Involve your family in your major decisions and communicate with them, especially if they will be affected by your decision. If a decision affects you, it will likely affect your loved ones somehow, too. You will find that their support is helpful and that it can alleviate some of your stress and worry.

De-Stress

Earlier, I mentioned an influential study on decision-making while under the influence of stress. The main finding of this study was that stress impairs your ability to make good decisions. Removing stress from the equation is helpful in reaching a satisfactory decision.

When faced with a decision, you need to remove stress. Unfortunately, decisions often put additional stress on you. It is best to remove any additional stress by removing yourself from the situation around you. Go somewhere quiet, even just the bathroom. Take a few moments to breathe deeply. You can even try using a stress ball or Chinese meditation balls to help still the racing thoughts in your mind. If you can take some time to really consider all of your options, then do so. But time is not always available, so make the best of the time that you do have. You can effectively remove stress from your mind in just a few minutes by yourself.

Chapter 4: The Art of Making Snap Decisions

Snap decisions do not give you the time you need to debate each option carefully. They require you to be quick-witted and decisive. The pressure of time is often stressful. It is helpful to use the tips covered in the previous chapter when making a snap decision. However, for the sake of speed, consider some of these additional tips as well.

Decide by Rote

Expert intuition arises when you become familiar with something. It is easy to make decisions when you are familiar with the circumstances. If you are faced with quick decisions in the workplace, often time your training will be enough to help you hone your expert intuition into something that you can use to make decisions. Once you have expert intuition, it is easy to make decisions without wavering. Always use your expert intuition and do not waste time doubting yourself.

Expert intuition does not just apply to work. Think of situations that you have become accustomed to in life. You have developed a certain expert intuition for many scenarios based on your life experience. Rely on this intuition to help you make expedient decisions at the snap of your fingers.

Use a Deadline

Set deadlines for yourself. Two minutes is usually sufficient for a snap decision. You must make up your mind by your deadline. Once time is up, time is up. You cannot extend your deadline. This pressure can help you think more quickly.

Pick a Random Decision

If all decisions seem equal in pros and cons, just pick one at random. You can flip a coin, draw from a hat, or just mentally pick a decision. But you do not need to develop analysis paralysis by thinking too much or too hard. You need to just take action. Only use this method when you are truly unable to decide because all decisions seem equal.

Accept that Failure is Possible

It is possible to make the wrong decision. Do not worry too much about that. In the moment of a snap decision, you don't have time to deliberate and worry. You just need to take decisive action. Understand that this can lead to poor judgment. But you really have no choice when you have to act fast.

Think in Black and White

Limit your choices. Think in terms of black and white. Is something good or bad? Is something helpful or unhelpful? Un-complicate things drastically by thinking in simpler terms and cutting out certain decisions that just do not seem to make sense.

It is OK to be honest and ruthless when making a quick decision, as well. Do not sit there and worry about how other people will feel. Just make the best decision at hand. Worry about feelings and other less important sentiments later on.

Set Clear Criteria

Set very clear, undebatable criteria for each decision that you make. Understand the decision and the desired outcome. Compare each option to your list of criteria. The most qualified option is that one that you should pick. Your criteria is not variable; it must be concrete.

Limit Emotion

Snap decisions cannot be fraught with emotion. Emotions can cloud your judgment and catch you in a trap of confusion. You want to satisfy your feelings, yet you also want to serve the greater good. Avoid this trap by focusing on concrete, material benefits, rather than the

emotional aspects of decisions.

Visualize Results

If you are still having trouble determining

which option is ideal, take a moment to visualize

the results of each option. You can probably

determine the effects of each option based on life

experience. Go with the option that offers the

best foreseeable outcome.

Chapter 5: How to Be Resolute in your Decisions

When you make a decision, it can be tempting to flip-flop on your resolve. You may worry that you have made the wrong choice, and you feel eager to change your mind right away. Indecision still extends after you have made a decision, and it adds a great deal of unpleasantness and chaos to your life.

You create a great deal of strife and instability for yourself if you keep changing your mind about things. You start to organize your life around a particular decision that you have made, and then suddenly you change your mind. You must scramble to change everything.

In addition, you do not look very good to others when you are unable to stick to your original decisions. You can look weak and fickle if you are always changing your mind. People will no longer be able to rely on your judgment or stability.

For these reasons, it is critical that you stop this habit of flip-flopping on decisions. Once you make a decision, you must be resolute. Do not waver. When you make a decision, you need to make it swiftly and firmly. Consider yourself as an authority and trust in your own judgment. This can be very hard if you have little confidence, but sometimes faking confidence can make you become more confident over time. You will become more respected and your life will be easier. You will also probably respect yourself more if you become more resolute in your decisions.

Live with the Results

Live with the results. You can change them if you must. But being final in your decisions can help you make sure that a decision is right or wrong. Things are often stressful at first; it can be easy to think you made the wrong choice. Unless you are totally certain that something is the wrong choice, however, stick with a decision. With time, it may just start to work out.

Put Aside Unimportant Distractions

It is easy to get distracted from your resolves. Little things seem appealing and make you question your decision. But you should not chase after little things. You made your decision for a reason. You will probably be making a huge mistake by changing your mind based on trivial things.

For instance, say you married your spouse because you love him or her. But now some cute new co-worker is distracting you with constant flirting. This little distraction may make you waver in your loyalty, but ultimately flirtation is not worth sacrificing the sanctity of your marriage.

Keep Your Word

Say you suddenly desire to change your mind. Consider if you will be letting anyone down when you do this. Will you be breaking any promises? If so, you should avoid changing your mind. Keep your word always. This will make you a better person, and it will lead to other people trusting in you more.

Remember All of Your Efforts

You probably put a lot of work into a decision. This work does not just mean nothing. It is valuable time that you invested in something. Therefore, it would be a shame to throw all of your work away because you changed your mind.

Know when to Change

Sometimes, being resolute is not helpful. You absolutely must change your mind in some situations. Learn to recognize when a decision you make is just not working out, no matter how hard you try to make it work. Realize that sometimes you just have to give up and move on to something better. There is no shame in admitting defeat if you are improving a situation by doing so.

Chapter 6: How to Make Major Life Decisions Easy

Sometimes, you find yourself faced with cripplingly huge decisions. Your life or death may hang in the balance. The life or death of a loved one may be at stake. Your entire financial future may hinge on one decision. These huge decisions are so hard because they have huge, far-reaching implications for your entire life. In addition, you cannot see into the mists of the future enough to know exactly which decision is best. All of your options may seem equally beneficial and detrimental, creating a very conflicting and difficult decision making process.

Typically, you cannot just run and hide from major life decisions. You have to take action. But that can be very hard. You may be completely clueless about what to do and which of your options you should choose. So what do you do?

Deeply Explore Your Values

The great thing about a major life decision is that it is entirely yours to make. You are in control. You can get to know yourself and make a decision based on your true values and beliefs.

You should first consider both decisions and their implications for your values. Let's say you are trying to choose between two jobs. One job lets you get that nice house you wanted because it pays more; the other job means that you have to stay in a little apartment, but you have more time to spend with your young children. Well, both options are appealing. But which means more to you, having a nice family home or spending time with your kids before they grow up? Most people would probably choose the latter, but there is truly no right or wrong answer. You should choose which value means more to you and make the decision based on which job satisfies your values the most.

Discard Irrelevant Beliefs

Many people stick to certain decisions because they believe (erroneously) that a certain decision will lead them to their future goals. They put aside their wants and needs now for some future goal. While it is great to think of the long-term, you should also ask yourself if you really are benefiting the long-term. Is your current decision really going to bring you closer to your goals? Or is there a better path?

A good example is if you choose to pursue a certain degree or course of study that you hate, in the hope of one day achieving your dream career. Do you really need that degree to get your dream job? In some cases, yes, you do. But in some cases, work experience, leadership skills, and sense means more than a degree. You do not need an MBA to open your dream business, for instance. Really look into your dream career and determine if you really need to stick with a horrible degree and four or more years in school to get it.

Another example is if you take a job you hate because you think it will help you advance to a more coveted position. Sometimes, you do have to endure some time in a crappy job to attain your goals. But sometimes you don't have to. Again, you should carefully look into what you really need to attain the position you really want.

Listen to Your Intuition

I discussed the three types of intuition before. When making major life decisions, you probably have a preference deep in your gut. It is a choice that you just naturally prefer. But you push down your gut instinct out of fear that it is incorrect. You raise all sorts of concerns and basically argue with yourself about what is really best.

Stop doing this. Trust your intuition when it comes to decisions that profoundly affect your life. You know what you really want and need deep inside your brain and your gut. Your subconscious mind already knows what the best decision is, so listen to it. It will guide you in the ideal direction.

Put Your Happiness First

Your happiness is important, no matter what other people say. When making a major life decision, consider which decision offers you more happiness and a greater quality of life. This can be hard, especially when you are faced with a medical or financial decision where no options seem to make you happy. Nevertheless, one option probably offers greater quality of life in some way. Which decision will offer you the most security and peace of mind? Which carries the least risk? Which will harm you and your loved ones the least? This is the decision you should probably make, because it will bring more happiness in the long run.

Often, people neglect their happiness because they assume that things like wealth, job security, or health will result in happiness in the future. But consider how happy you are if you make a lot of money but are too busy all the time to ever enjoy spending it? Money and other material considerations are rarely more important than your ultimate happiness right now. This goes back to my point about exploring your values. Do not wait to achieve happiness at a later date because of material yield. Instead, do what makes you happy now.

Accept that there are No Bad Decisions

While it may not seem like it when you are in the middle of wrestling with a huge life decision, there are really no bad decisions. You can make a poor decision, but you will be able to recover from it and make another decision in the future. Some things that seem monumental now will not matter so much in the future, so understand that whatever happens is just a part of life. One day it will not matter so much.

Most likely, nothing is black or white. Whatever decision you make will offer you some good and some bad. You will not throw your life away with one decision or the other. You will simply shape your fate.

Think this way to remove the stress from life decisions. If you do not consider things in black and white, you can feel less panic at the face of a monumental life decision. You can approach decisions from a more rational angle, than an emotionally charged, frightened angle. You will relieve yourself of a lot of stress, which you by now know is a major no-no when making decisions. You need to clear the stress away in order to make a good decision.

Talk It Over

When you are making a major life decision, what you decide impacts everyone around you, not just you. Your family members and friends will feel the results of your decision. Your family and friends also know you well and they can offer you intimate and accurate outside perspectives. Therefore, it is a good idea to use the support of your family and friends when making life decisions. Use their counsel to make the best choice for yourself.

Some major life decisions also involve your loved ones. In these cases, your loved ones should all work together as a team to reach a decision together. Facilitate the decision making process by leading discussions with all of your loved ones and guiding the process in healthy directions. You can help your loved ones use the skills that you have learned in this book when they are all trying to come up with the best decision or solution for a problem.

Chapter 7: Taking Charge as a Leader

Leaders are charged with the crucial task of making decisions, often several a day. People rely upon you to lead them to success, which means that you must make decisions for many people. Making a bad decision could result in great failure for everyone. Talk about pressure. You have to know how to make good decisions if you are a good leader.

Decision making skills are especially useful at work. If you can demonstrate sound decision-making, you become eligible for leadership positions. You can become a candidate for managerial positions and other such leadership positions. Developing these skills not only makes your work easier, but it can help advance your career. Good decisions-making skills will transform you from a good employee to a great one.

Taking charge and being a leader can be very useful in your love life, as well. All of your personal relationships can benefit from certain levels of leadership. Women especially love a man who can lead. Men who make executive decisions without hesitation project confidence, which is naturally appealing to women. Being able to take the lead and make decisions can help direct your relationships and make you the dominant partner.

Making leadership decisions is absolutely and undoubtedly necessary when you are a parent. You are acting as a leader to your children. You must guide them to become great adults. You can only do this by making decisions that are crucial for their health, wellness, happiness, and ultimate formation.

It is time to learn to put aside indecision and take charge as a leader. The following tips will help you become the type of leader who is respected for his or her decision making skills. These tips will benefit all areas of your life and help you reach greatness through well-made decisions.

Understand the Importance of Your Decisions

As a leader, each decision you make is very important. This is because your decisions do not just impact you. They impact all of the people that you are in charge of. Your team at work, your family, your friendly bowling league – these are all groups of people that you can impact with your decisions as a leader. Understanding the importance of your decisions can make decisions daunting. But it can also make you feel more motivated to make the right decision.

Believe in yourself as a leader. You are now a leader for a reason. People trust your judgment and look up to you. Use this to calm your nerves when you are afraid of letting everyone down. You have more sense than you realize, and you are capable of making great leadership decisions.

Find Your Leadership Dimension

There are eight leadership dimensions. Good leaders will adopt all eight dimensions in their leadership styles. However, most people have one or two dimensions that they prefer and act the strongest in. Understanding all of the dimensions helps you see how you are as a leader and what dimensions you are best at using in your leading skills. Then you can understand how to approach decision making in a way that is natural for you. You will have less difficulty making decisions if you undertake decision making without having to change yourself in any way. You can also see other dimensions and forms of decision-making that you should strengthen yourself in.

There are eight dimensions of leadership. Read on to see which dimension you fit into and how that impacts your decision-making abilities.

Pioneering – A pioneering leader tries new things. He is revolutionary and not content with the status quo. He goes out of his way to bring change and new experiences to his team. He is bold and likes to try risks.

You can benefit from snappy decision making if you are this type of leader, but you should take care not to be overly impulsive. Do not let a fear of losing power make you commit to decisions that are not healthy for the whole team, just out of stubbornness.

Energizing – An energizing leader is focused on helping his team feel motivated. He provides motivation and encouragement in generous helpings. He likes to see progress. Final decision making is crucial in this type of leadership.

You want to make decisions that benefit your entire team, and then stick with them for the greater good of everyone. Take your time and use your team's input to make decisions. Do not worry about not being liked, however. Your job as a leader is not to be liked. Rejection is another common fear of energizing leaders. Do not let that get to you. You are a leader, so your word should be accepted.

Affirming – An affirming leader is like a best friend, who uses his closeness with each individual team member to bond the team as a cohesive whole. He leads through friendship, gentleness, and kindness. He is not an authoritarian boss. These types of leaders must implement decisions that make everyone feel included and valued so as to preserve the friendship.

If you are an affirming leader, you hate pressuring others and you worry that your team members may get hostile with you. But sometimes you need to deal with hostility and up the pressure on your subordinates when you are a leader. Stop letting fear get in the way of your decisions. Your word is the final decision and other people have to respect that. Do not let others or fear of displeasing others rule your decisions in any way.

Inclusive – An inclusive leader includes everyone in the team as equals. Everyone must work equally hard. The leader will go out of his way to accommodate people who may not be able to join in. Therefore, he must take the reins when making decisions and he must make decisions that sometimes appear to favor certain people. In reality, he is not showing favoritism at all, but is simply working to be inclusive of everyone in the team regardless of their abilities. He fears letting people down, so he strives not to when he makes decisions.

Take some of the pressure off of yourself if you are an inclusive leader. You are not letting everyone down if you make a single mistake. Don't let fear cripple you when making decisions.

Humble – A humble leader is calm, measured, and unemotional. He has an even temperament. He likes to take his time and be as reliable as possible. He hates being pressured by time and he hates overly emotional situations.

When making a decision as a humble leader, you must accept that sometimes emotions will run high and sometimes time will be a constraint. As much as you hate these things, use your deliberation and emotional calm as an edge over others when you make a decision. You have the skills to remove stress from your mind as you try to reach a proper decision because you are naturally prone to being calm. Do not let pressure add stress and drama to your decision-making.

Deliberate – A deliberate leader is an authoritarian leader who likes to be right. He likes to show off his expertise and use his skill sets to reach very helpful decisions. He is not fond of being challenged or being proved wrong.

While being deliberate is a good thing because it makes you a strong leader, you must not become too stubborn. If you make a mistake while deciding between different options, sometimes you will have to admit that you were wrong. It is human to be wrong. Then you can prove your expertise by rectifying your mistake. Fixing your mistakes rather than insisting that you were right will make your team respect you more.

Resolute – A resolute leader knows just what he wants. He sets high standards, and it crushes him when these standards are not met. He wants everything to run smoothly and he sees no reason why things should not work properly.

Decisions can be challenging for you when you demand so much perfection. You may worry that you are lowering your standards when you make a decision. Remove this worry and instead use your high standards as a useful criteria to base your decisions off of. Never compromise your standards, or you will feel guilty.

Commanding – This type of leader is driven by victory and results. He is commanding because he is so focused on the end goal. He is a strong leader, and he hates to appear weak.

It is OK to look past the end result sometimes. It is also not a sign of weakness to admit that you made a wrong decision or to rely on the input of others to reach a major decision. Sometimes you need help, but this help only makes you stronger. You can achieve your dreams of victory if you work with your team to reach big decisions.

Take Advantage of Your Position

If you are in a leadership position, you should take full advantage of your authority. It is up to you to make decisions. You have the final voice in all decisions. You should not let other people take your position away from you.

This does not imply that you should ignore the input of your team members. A good leader uses the input and advice of the whole team to arrive at decisions. A good leader leads his team to success; he is not some dictator who leads the team only in the direction that he wants. However, being a leader means that you have the ultimate say. Use your team for input and guide everyone under your leadership toward success, but keep the ultimate authority for yourself.

It is certainly a great idea to use consensus decision making when you are a leader. This is when the entire family votes on where to go for dinner, or a team votes on the best strategy to adopt for the completion of a project. You still have the ultimate say, however, and you can influence the voting as well.

It is your prerogative to be a commanding leader if you need to be. In some circumstances, such as during emergencies, it is essential to be commanding because there is not time for collaborating and voting on a decision. Someone has to take charge, and if that person is you, then do not feel guilt or shame in calling the shots without the input of others. Usually, though, this is not the best leadership style. You can quickly become cold and unavailable to your team's individual needs if you always assume the commanding position.

Understand that You Won't Please Everyone

Sometimes, the decisions you make will upset people. People will not agree with your decisions. But do not let people inject fear or doubt into you, especially if you are a humble, inclusive, or affirming leader who fears being rejected and stuck in emotionally charged situations. You are the leader and other people are not always able to understand why you made the choices that you have. However, you have everyone's best interests at heart. You made your decision for a reason. You saw the long-term and benefits that others may not see. Just stick by your decision, and do not give into the hostility and aggression of others.

Do not let fear of what other people will say or think influence your decisions, either. People may be upset at first, but they will probably get over it in time when they see that you were actually right.

When someone injects doubt into you, ask yourself how qualified that person is to be making decisions in your place. Perhaps this person does add valuable input. In that case, it is useful to take his objections into consideration. However, if someone does not offer much usefulness as a leader, then his input on decisions should not have too much bearing on what you ultimately decide.

Focus on the Long-term and the Greater Good

It can make some individual people upset, but focusing on the greater good of the majority is important when you are working as a leader of a team. The majority usually has more influence and therefore it should have more bearing on your decisions. What benefits the most people is important to always consider when making a decision as a leader. Always ask yourself, what will bring about the most good for the most people?

In addition, the long-term is often better to consider than the short-term. Short-term solutions only add more problems if they do not consider long-term effects. Focusing on the short-term is why many projects and businesses fail. Always consider the future and the ultimate results of each decision, rather than the short-term results. Some decisions will solve problems that your team faces immediately, but will not solve long-term issues. Some decisions may benefit your current problems right now, but will lead to greater problems later in the future. Avoid decisions that neglect to take care of the future. Thinking that you can make a short-term decision and then fix all of the subsequent problems that this decision causes sometime in the future is not an ideal strategy to follow. You should never put off taking care of impending issues, as they will probably worsen with time.

Follow Ethics

When making decisions as a leader, it is important to always follow ethics. Ethics ensure that you take care of the feelings and human rights of everyone involved. Creating an ethical environment is one of your duties as a leader. By doing so, you create a team that cares about the good of others, and avoids performing harmful actions. While there are many ethics to consider as a leader, here are some main ones that you should consider when you are trying to make a decision.

Keep Promises – Did you make a promise or commitment to someone or something? If so, try to make decisions that honor your promise. If you break a promise, you can hurt yourself, as well as the people that you are breaking the promise too. You want to be an honest, trustworthy leader, and one way to do this is to stick to the promises and commitments that you make. Consider promises binding and do all that you can to keep them.

Don't Lie – Deceit is never ethical. Does a decision call for you to employ deceit in any way? Are you duping anyone with a certain decision? If so, then that choice is probably not the best one to make.

Remember the Golden Rule – Always remember the Golden Rule, "Treat others as you would want to be treated." If you make decisions that disrespect or hurt others in a way that you would not tolerate, then you are violating a major ethic. You are also likely to lose favor with the majority, which is never desirable, especially when you are in a leadership position.

Don't Blame Others – Do not blame other people for your mistakes or problems. Make decisions that further the greater good; do not make decisions to punish or otherwise blame other people.

Avoid Favoritism – Favoritism is never helpful in any situation because it breeds resentment within your team. It is best to avoid favoritism at all costs. Make decisions that are unbiased toward particular people. Favoritism is unfortunately a part of human nature; there will be team members that you prefer over and get along with better than others. But always strive to be impartial and to never indicate any of your personal preferences or feelings toward others.

Operate within the Law – This one is obvious. Unless you want to go to jail, it is best to operate within the law. Do not make decisions that call for you to engage in illegal activity. The laws are in place for a reason, to keep order in society, and so you can avoid much trouble by following them.

Minimize Hardships for Others – Each decision you make should aim to minimize hardship and suffering for everyone involved. While you should focus on the greater good, do not sacrifice the good of some people just to please the majority. Always think of the good of all of your team members. Strive to avoid causing anybody any kind of harm.

Strive to Make Things Better – With each decision you make, your ultimate goal should be to make your organization or environment better in some way. You should make decisions that benefit the ultimate good and bring about improvements. Look for ways to improve your organization or environment, and then work to make those improvements. Consider how each of your options will help you make a positive improvement to your current situation.

Chapter 8: In Conclusion

In the past, indecisiveness may have plagued you. Making decisions was a challenging process that inspired dread in you. You used to feel overwhelmed when you had to make any kind of choice. Even choosing a dish at a restaurant or a pair of shoes at a store may have been an agonizing ordeal for you.

But now, you are fortified with some better skills for making decisions. From the important to the trivial, you can make decisions with more comfort and ease. This book offers you the peace and the resolution that you need to impose order and stability in your life with some good decisions.

You now know to relax and minimize stress. Stress kills your ability to make wise choices, so you should avoid it at all costs while you are engaged in the decision-making process. You also know how to think about decisions in a more positive, constructive way. Decisions can no longer make you quake with fear because you know how to have a better relationship with the whole process.

The work that goes into decisions is easier when you are not scrambling around in a panic, trying to find the very best choice that will save the entire world. It is far better to take a breath, get an objective opinion, and sketch a decision tree or some other list. Use some strategies to arrive at good decisions, rather than floundering with too many thoughts bombarding your brain.

The skills and strategies in this book are excellent for making good decisions.

You also know the different factors that should influence your decisions. Instead of making decisions for all of the wrong reasons, you now know how to make them for all the right ones. You understand how to apply ethical considerations to your decisions. You know to focus on the long-term objectives and the great good of the majority. You know that you should strive for the betterment of life and others through your decisions.

With all of this knowledge, you are equipped to begin making good decisions without as much strife or confusion. You are now in a position to become a strong leader. You are now able to hold the appropriate control over your own life. Indecisiveness is no longer the horrible affliction that you must struggle with every day over the littlest things. The peace that you can now enjoy is amazing.

Other great books by Madison Taylor on Kindle, paperback and audio

Rejection Proof Therapy 101: How To Overcome, Deal With And Heal Yourself From Rejection

Cognitive Behavioral Therapy For Beginners: How To Use CBT To Overcome Anxieties, Phobias, Addictions, Depression, Negative Thoughts, And Other Problematic Disorders

Forbidden Psychology 101: The Cool Stuff They Didn't Teach You About In School

Escaping the Introvert World: The Introvert's Guide To Overcoming Shyness, Social Anxiety, And Fear To Thrive In An Extrovert World

NLP For Beginners: Learn the Secrets of Self Mastery, Developing Magnetic Influence and Reaching Your Goals Using Neuro-Linguistic Programming

Depression Proof Yourself: How To Avoid And Overcome Being Depressed

Love Thyself: The First Commandment to Raising your Self Esteem, Boosting your Self-Confidence, and Increasing your Happiness

Sources

Brandeis University Graduate Professional
Studies. (2016). *Leadership and Decision
      Making*. Retrieved from
http://projectmgmt.brandeis.
edu/resources/articles/leadership-and-decision-
making/.

Schwartz, B. (2004). *The Paradox of Choice:
Why Less is More*. Ecco Publishing: New
      York, NY.

Sugarman, J., Scullard, M., & Wilhelm, E. (2011).
*The 8 Dimensions of Leadership:
      DiSC Strategies for Becoming a Better
Leader*. Brett-Koehler Publishers: San
      Francisco, CA.

Milton Keynes UK
Ingram Content Group UK Ltd.
UKHW040103120824
1226UKWH00019B/6

9 781540 305527